# Antique and Collectible
# Marbles
## Third Edition

## by Everett Grist

**COLLECTOR BOOKS**
*A Division of Schroeder Publishing Co., Inc.*

To Goldie. . .

who puts up with my collecting habits;
who also enjoys having these little baubles around for awhile;
and who then joins me in passing them on to other marble lovers.

Additional copies of this book may be ordered from:

Everett Grist
P.O. Box 91375
Chattanooga, Tennessee 37412

COLLECTOR BOOKS
P.O. Box 3009
Paducah, Kentucky 42002-3009
www.collectorbooks.com

Copyright © 1992 Everett Grist

The current values in this book should be used only as a guide. They are not intended to set prices, which vary from one section of the country to another. Auction prices as well as dealer prices vary greatly and are affected by condition as well as demand. Neither the authors nor the publisher assumes responsibility for any losses that might be incurred as a result of consulting this guide.

Searching For A Publisher?

We are always looking for people knowledgeable within their fields. If you feel that there is a real need for a book on your collectible subject and have a large comprehensive collection, contact Collector Books.

# ACKNOWLEDGMENTS

I want to take this opportunity to extend my heartiest thanks to Wayne Sanders of Jefferson City, Missouri. Wayne is the proud owner of the two Comic-type marbles, the Tom Mix and the Cotes Big Loaf advertising marble. He was kind enough to send photographs to be included in this book.

The balance of the collection pictured is owned by Mr. Earl Hogue who lives near Cincinnati, Ohio. Earl was kind (and trusting!) enough to let us have his collection transported to Paducah, Kentucky, where the photographic session could be supervised by editors at Collector Books involved in the publication of this book.

A book would not be complete without saying a public "Thanks" to those who have provided a need for the book itself... the collectors of marbles everywhere.

Since the publication of the first edition, I have received many photographs of beautiful and rare marbles for which I am most grateful (warning: I do not return photos). Without this first-hand knowledge, it would be hard to believe that such a large variety exists. I will include as many as possible in this edition, but take into consideration that marbles are usually much prettier than the pictures. Marbles are hard to photograph and our editor is very particular. Many of the rarest ones are left out because of poor quality of the photographs.

I now have the world's largest collection of photographs of marbles. My next book (I am working on it at this time) will contain many of these photos.

**Following is a list of collectors and/or dealers interested in buying who also often have marbles for sale. I believe them to be trustworthy and fair dealers.**

## Collectors

Frank M. Gardenhire
3608 Koons Road
Chattanooga, TN 37412
(423)867-5440

Jim and Louise O'Connell
5309 Wright
Troy, MI 48098
(810)879-0438

Mark Howard
6756 Perry Penny Dr.
Annandale, VA 22003
(703)642-5334

Gary and Sally Dolly
Box 2044
New Smyrna Beach, FL 32070

Brian Estepp
10380 Taylor Rd. S.W.
Reynoldsburg, OH 43068
(614)863-5350

Lloyd & Chris Huffer
Star Route
Damascus, PA 18415
(717)224-4012

## Collectors/Dealers

Wayne E. Sanders
2202 Livingston St.
Jefferson City, MO 65101
(314)636-7515

Stanely A. Block
51 Johnson St.
Trumbull, CT 06611
(203)261-3223 (After 6 p.m. weekdays)

Bill Sweet
P.O. Box 4736
Rumford, RI 02916
(401)434-4548

## Glass Grinders/Marble Restorers

Jack Leslie
Rt. 4 Box 60
Liberty, MO 64068
(816)455-2110

Larry Castle
885 Taylor Ave.
Ogden, UT 84404
(801)393-8131

## Clubs
**Please contact for informantion on marble meets and membership**

Marbles Unlimited
P.O Box 206
Northboro, MA 01532

Marble Collector's Society of America
P.O. Box 222
Trumbull, CT 06611

National Marble Club of America
440 Eaton Road
Drexel Hill, PA 19026

Buckeye Marble Collectors Club
437 Meadowbrook Drive
Newark, OH 43055

Southern California Marble Club
18361-1 Strothern Street
Reseda, CA 91335

# MAY I BLOW MY OWN HORN?

"What makes you think you are qualified to set the value on all these marbles?" I was asked. "Experience," I replied.

What else but experience could qualify a man to value or appraise anything? I would like to tell you all my experiences of the last four years but that would make another much larger book. In the last four years, I have driven over 300,000 miles and made several plane trips. I have displayed in or attended over 200 antique shows, flea markets or auctions (yes, that averages more than one a week). I have bought 12 major marble collections. I have had five auctions where nothing but marbles and related items were sold – all belonging to Goldie and me. For the first three of the last four years, not a week passed that I did not buy, sell, inspect or appraise anywhere from a few marbles to a large collection. My past experience as an antique dealer, show promoter and auctioneer has also helped. This has given me much pleasure and I thank my God that I have been able – both physically and financially – to pursue this endeavor. Keep in mind if I want to stay healthy and get along with my good wife, Goldie, I have to turn enough profit to at least meet expenses.

Now don't take this as a swan song – I am still in there. I no longer appraise for a fee, although I will give you a free oral appraisal when convenient. I do not sell by mail or from my home. I do sell at some shows and flea markets and I hope to have a few more auctions. I still have lots of marbles but all of the best are long gone. I need to buy and can pay a good price for good and rare marbles. I am also interested in large collections containing at least a few good ones.

I am always glad to hear from you and will try to answer your questions, but don't expect more than a couple of sentences. Please, to save time and expense, enclose a self-addressed, stamped envelope. You see, I am getting old and don't have a lot of time left – to waste that is.

Happy Hunting,
Everett Grist

# TABLE OF CONTENTS

# HOW IT ALL BEGAN

Why did it take us so long to realize how interesting marbles are! I have been exposed to them since early childhood. I can remember my older brother having a large German Swirl when we were children, given to him by our uncle. It was not to play with but we could take it out of the trunk occasionally to admire for awhile. But then it was wrapped again in tissue paper, put back in the box and placed back into the trunk for safe keeping.

I have bought many estates over the years, and have often found a Sulphide or two and sometimes some Swirls. However, I can't remember ever selling one for over $5.00 until a few years ago. Goldie and I were riding along in our pickup on our way home from an antique show in Michigan. We had been on a combination trip of making a show and visiting my mother and sister and Goldie's brother, which we did as often as possible. I had bought a fruit jar full of marbles for $20.00 from an old gentleman who had brought them into the show and offered them for sale. I didn't know much about marbles, but I had discovered there were some people who would pay as much as 50 or 75 cents for some of the Swirl marbles that had rough spots on opposite ends.

Somehow in packing, the jar was put up in the cab with us. Goldie, bored to death as usual on the long ride, had opened the jar and was looking at the marbles. "Look here," she said, "here is a little blue marble with silver flakes in it and a green one and a clear one. Have you ever seen anything like this before?" Well I hadn't or at least never paid any attention to it before. She looked all the marbles over carefully and even found a tiny one less than a half inch in diameter with two gold streaks in it. The marbles were soon forgotten and we went on with our regular routine.

Our next show was in Kansas City and while unpacking, the marbles turned up again. After getting everything set up, I sat down and started pricing the marbles - 50 and 75 cents on the Swirls and $1.00 on each of the silver flakes and the gold streak one. Goldie was out looking at the other booths to see what everybody else had. Before long, she came back and said there was a couple in a booth down at the other end of the building that had marbles similar to ours but their prices were much higher. I finished whatever I was doing at the time and, without any haste whatsoever, strolled on down to the booth as directed to check it out. Well, I was never so surprised in all my life. They were asking as much as $15.00 for some of the small marbles. I went back to the booth and told Goldie that I had never heard of such a thing and that they must be collectors who didn't really want to sell which would account for their marbles being priced so high. However, I did raise all my prices. The Swirls to $1.00, the ones with the silver flakes to $2.00, and the tiny little one with the gold streaks all the way up to $6.00. (By that time I had begun to like it myself.)

Nothing happened to the marbles the first day, but on the evening of the second day, Phil and Sarah walked in. They were looking for marbles and wanted to check out what we had. When Sarah saw my little one with gold streaks, she picked it up and the happiest look came over her face I have ever seen on a person. She bought it and Phil bought all the rest of the marbles, except the clays, the Benningtons and machine-made marbles, for a total somewhere in the neighborhood of $50.00, giving me a nice profit on my investment. We talked a long time and they told me a lot about marble collecting – much more, in fact, than I could understand at the time. They returned the next day with the names and addresses of the two marble clubs and suggested I join both which I did almost immediately. We talked for a long time and parted with the promise that if I found anything rare or unusual I would get in touch with them.

That was the beginning of many happy meetings and much more business than I could expect you to believe – both buying and selling. They know that I must make a profit or I couldn't meet expenses. They also know that if I find anything that I think might be of interest to them, they will hear from me. Yes, it took a long time for us to find the right couple that would take the time to share their knowledge with an older couple and we will forever be grateful.

# VALUING MARBLES

The wise old coot who told me a few small chips really didn't hurt anything obviously had some chipped marbles for sale. Condition is of the utmost importance in evaluating a marble. An absolute "mint" marble, that is one without a chip, a fracture, a crack, frosting or a manufacturer's defect which would take away from the beauty of the marble, is rare indeed. In my opinion, it is worth three to five times the value of a marble of the same type in "near mint" condition; that is, with only a small amount of any of the defects mentioned. It is the old story of supply and demand. There are many more collectors who are constantly looking for the better and rarer marbles to purchase, so as to upgrade their collection, than there are those who are willing to pay a fair price for a marble in less than perfect shape or "near mint."

The next grade is "good," which is a catch-all category that includes the rarer marbles with large chips, fractures and cracks, and polished marbles. In my opinion, the "good" grade is worth one half or less the value of the "near mint" marble of the same type. Swirls of the more common variety should not be included in this category but should be laid to rest, as they often distract rather than add to the beauty of the

7

collection. As for polished marbles, there are many different and varied opinions; but I believe they are generally being accepted by more people as having a place in a collection, especially the rarer and harder-to-find ones. It has been said that polishing a marble does not hurt the value of it. That is true, I am sure, with individual marbles. In fact, I have seen marbles before and after polishing and the process had increased the beauty ten fold; and then others did not turn out so well. The question is often asked, "Should I have this marble polished?" I am of the opinion that if the marble looks good in its present condition, even if you can display only one side without distraction, leave it alone, as far as resale is concerned. If the next guy wants it polished, let him have it done. Of course, if it is a sorry looking lot in its present condition, why not? Polishing is not expensive and you may get a pleasant surprise – I have many times. So as I see it, there need only be three grades: 1. Absolute "mint" which can vary only to a very small degree. 2. "Near mint" which might vary more. 3. "Good" or "collectible" which can vary a great deal according to the rarity of the marble.

# PRICING

The values I am listing are for marbles in "average near mint" condition, 1¾" on sulphides, ¾" and 1¾" on the others. Sulphides 1" and under are worth slightly more and over 2¼" much more. Swirls ½" and under are worth slightly more and the rarer types 2" and larger, considerably more. These are the retail prices I would ask if I owned these marbles in "average near mint" condition. Of course, in pricing your marbles, you must take into consideration even in "near mint" marbles, some are "nearer mint" than others and in the "good" grade, some are better than others.

# TRANSPARENT SWIRL

The first class of marbles is the Transparent Swirl. They are divided into six sub-classes: Solid Core, Latticino Core, Divided Core, Ribbon Core, Lobed Core and Coreless. The first listed is the Solid Core.

The Solid Core Swirls are made of transparent glass, usually clear, with a core that is solid opaque. It is sometimes solid white and other times striped and swirled. The most common colors are red and white (but sometimes only red or white), red, white and blue and sometimes red, white and green. It is usually decorated nearer the surface with other color lines or ribbons and sometimes both.

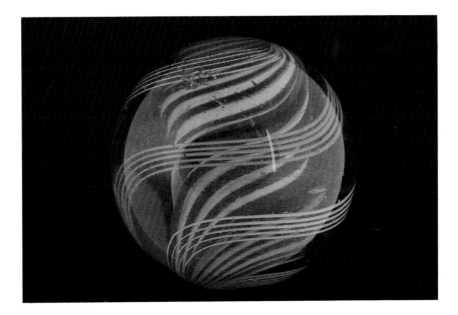

The second sub-class is the Divided Core Swirls. They are of transparent glass, usually clear. The center of the marble is clear surrounded by a number of colored glass ribbons. They vary tremendously in number, color and shape. There is usually another decoration of thin threads nearer the surface; sometimes singular, at other times in groups of two, three and four.

The third sub-class is Latticino Core Swirls. They are clear glass with a core of small threads of glass that usually are either yellow or white. I have never seen any other color, but have heard of a few red ones. The number of threads vary from eight to 30 or 40. There is always another decoration of various colors of ribbons either on or near the surface. These probably are the most common of the Swirl marbles.

The fourth sub-class of the Transparent Swirl marbles is the Ribbon Core. They are made of transparent glass, usually clear. In the center is a single ribbon that usually swirls one time around, sometimes more, from end to end. There is usually other decoration in the form of lines or ribbons or both which are nearer the surface. This seems to be the rarest and therefore the most valuable or desirable of the Swirls.

Sub-class five, Lobed Core Swirl, is transparent glass, usually clear. In the center is a solid opaque core that looks much like the solid core. Upon close examination, you will discover it has lobes, most often four. These lobes usually do not swirl, although some marbles are found in which the lobes are swirled. There is usually a small amount of decoration near the surface.

Coreless Swirls, as we speak of them here, are marbles made of transparent glass, usually clear, but also often colored. They always have outer decoration of stripes or ribbons on or near the surface. They are usually of the smaller size, seldom measuring more than 1". With a few exceptions, they are not very pretty and therefore the least desirable of the Transparent Swirls. Although this photo shows three sizes of marbles, they vary only slightly in size, from slightly under ¾" to slightly over ¾".

Transparent Swirl. This is a fine example of a Ribbon Core and is an extra nice marble.

Transparent Swirl. A fine example of the Solid Core.

Transparent Swirl. Another fine example of the Solid Core.

Transparent Swirl. Four good examples of the Split or Divided Core.

# LUTZ

Lutz, or Lutz-type as some prefer, are the most important types of collectible marbles. I don't wish to get into the discussion here whether or not these are true Lutz or Lutz-types and whether or not they were all made by Lutz at the Boston and Sandwich factory; all I will say, if he did make them all, he sure was a busy little fellow. However, this type is so important in the marble-collecting world that I would like to divide them into seven different and distinct types.

Lutz-type one, Clear Swirl. This type is made of clear glass with two or three lines of white or colored glass on the surface running in a swirl from top to bottom and separated by two ribbons of gold-colored flakes that are usually outlined with threads of white glass. This is the least desirable of the Lutz-type, therefore the least expensive.

Lutz-type two, Colored Transparent Swirl, is the same as above except they are made from transparent colored glass, often blue or green and sometimes yellow.

Lutz-type three, Opaque Glass Swirls, is the same as above except they are made with opaque glass. These colors vary greatly. They have been found in different shades of blue, yellow, green, vaseline and even black; but are not to be confused with other black glass Lutz or the Indian Swirl Lutz.

The fourth type of Lutz is the Ribbon Core Lutz. It is made of clear or colored transparent glass with a thick ribbon of opaque glass, usually white but sometimes colored, running in swirls through the center of the marble and reaching from side to side. The outside of this ribbon reaches the surface, is covered with a ribbon of gold-colored flakes, and is outlined with a thread of white glass.

Lutz-type number five, Onionskin Lutz, is made the same as the Onionskin or Opaque Swirl described in another part of this book, except gold-colored flakes are added.

Lutz-type number six, Single Color Lutz is made of only one color glass and almost completely covered in streaks of gold-colored flakes. They are found in the colors black, green, white and I have seen one example of blue. Both the black glass and the green glass are pictured.

The Lutz-type seven, which is merely the Indian Swirl (described elsewhere in this book) with gold-colored flakes added.

Onionskin Lutz. This is the only one of this type I have seen. The streaks of gold are separated above the onionskin coloring.

Lutz. This is a close-up of the single color green Lutz mentioned earlier in group number six of Lutz-type marbles.

Lutz. Two Ribbon Core type marbles and one of the Clear Swirls mentioned elsewhere.

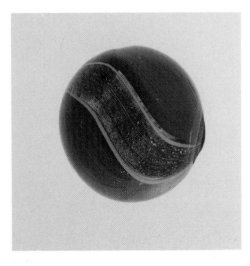

Ribbon Core Lutz. This is a very unusual marble and an extremely fine one.

Opaque Swirl Lutz. Though these are of black glass, these are not known as the black glass Lutz.

# PEPPERMINT SWIRLS

Peppermint Swirls. These sweet sounding Swirls are opaque glass of red, white and blue. They vary in layout but always have the same colors and are always opaque.

Peppermint Swirls with mica. Same as above with mica added to the blue strip or band. They are rare and very desirable, especially in the larger size.

Peppermint Swirl (left), Transparent Swirl Solid Core, Peppermint color (right). It has been reported that there has been much confusion about these two marble types, especially in the process of doing business by mail. We insert them here in hopes it will help eliminate the trouble.

# INDIAN SWIRL

Indian Swirls. These marbles are made of black glass with outer bands of colored glass that seem to have been applied to the surface. The width and density of these bands vary greatly and so do the colors. Note: not all black glass marbles are Indian Swirls. There is a long-running discussion as to where these marbles were made and how they got their name.

Right: 360° Indian Swirl, a very fine and rare example. Left: Joseph Swirl. Here I disagree with the Marble Collectors Society of America's glossary of terms. Mr. Paul Jones, formerly of Nashville, Tennessee, recently of California, called this type marble *Joseph Swirl* long before the M.C.S.A. came into being. I am old fashioned and proud of it. So, I must go along with Mr. Jones. Also, Randal & Webb in Greenberg's Guide to Marbles, page 23, center of picture shows an even finer example of a Joseph Swirl, which they call an Indian Swirl. In fact, I don't feel comfortable referring to any of the three marbles as Indian Swirls. Now I don't mean to criticize their book, I think it is a fine book over all, very well done. But, even I have not always been 100% right.

# BANDED OPAQUE SWIRL

Banded Opaque Swirls. These are made of opaque glass with wide bands that usually swirl from the top to the bottom. These bands are sometimes all of one color but often are of different colors. The base glass is often white but may be seen in several different colors, even an unusual opaque amber with red bands.

Banded Opaque. This is an unusually fine example.

# BANDED TRANSPARENT SWIRL

Banded Transparent Swirl. These are the same as the opaque except the base glass is transparent; sometimes clear, at other times colored. I don't remember ever seeing one of the transparent type which I thought was pretty. They have that "end-of-the-line", or the "last-of-the-batch" or the "let's-hurry-up-and-get-this-thing-through-with" look. They differ from the Coreless Swirls in that here we are dealing with bands which are wider than regular stripes or ribbons.

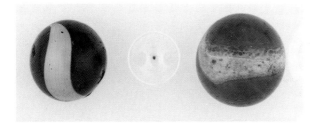

Left: Amber with yellow band. This is also a banded transparent swirl, but of a special type. I have seen this exact type & color from ½" to 1⅝" or that is, I have seen about ⅔ of one that would have been 1⅝" if it had all been there. It was in such bad condition that I did not buy it, but I wish I had bought it because I have not seen another over 1⅛". Although you see one occasionally, they are rare in any size. Right: a single pontil green with thin yellow band. It has a ground pontil much in the same manner as most sulphides. It has been suggested by more than one knowledgable collector that it was probably made by Mr. J. Harvey Leighton in Ohio circa 1900. I have no way of confirming it.

# ONIONSKIN

Onionskins are opaque marbles with a large core of clear glass which is covered with a thin layer of opaque glass, then covered again with a thin layer of clear glass. The colored glass is made up of lines or ribbons and bands of different colors. These ribbons and bands are spotted or mottled which gives the marble an overall mottled appearance. The colors are often in swirls, sometimes lobed. These marbles are usually large and are seldom found smaller than 1" with the mottled look. I believe this mottled look is necessary as far as quality is concerned in an Onionskin. Onionskins will also have two pontil marks. We know that the phrase *pontil mark* is technically wrong on two-pontiled marbles, because the marks were not made by a pontil rod but by marble scissors. However, the phrase is so entrenched and so in use by the marble collectors, we'll not try to change it, accepting it as truly meaning a marble scissors mark.

Onionskins.

Onionskin. This marble has 16 lobes and is a very unusual specimen.

Onionskin. This marble has unusual coloring.

Onionskin. This is an unusual four-lobed Onionskin.

Onionskin. This is a nice specimen.

Onionskin. Another nice specimen.

Onionskins with mica.

Onionskins with mica.

# OPAQUE SWIRL

The Opaque Swirl marbles present a small problem. This marble is listed by the Marble Collectors Society of America as an Onionskin and widely accepted by many collectors as such. However, having talked to many knowledgeable collectors who agree with me, I am going to try to establish a new category. We feel there is a definite difference in the marbles and I believe there is a need for a separation. The difference is that while the Onionskin has spots or a mottled look, there are no spots or mottled appearance to this marble. They are usually small in size and seldom found larger than 1". After examining many marbles, I have found that there are some which have an overall mottling and some with no spots at all and so these are easy to classify. But what about the ones that have mostly solid lines, ribbons and bands and with only a few spots? This I don't know; someone else will have to make the decision.

Opaque Swirls. Although this photo shows four different sizes, they vary only slightly from just under to just over ¾".

# END OF DAY

End of Day. This marble looks like the Onionskin except it has only one pontil mark. I do not believe this is a marble from the end of the cane as is sometimes claimed, but that the one true pontil mark indicates that they were individually made marbles.

# CLAMBROTH

Clambroth. These are made of opaque glass, usually white although any color might be used as long as it is opaque, and covered with thin lines of colored glass evenly spaced in a swirl from top to bottom. Often only two colors are used in the swirls, but sometimes as many as four different colors are used alternately in the lines. In marbles where black or a dark colored glass was used for the base, white threads were used. Clambroth is the second most important marble to advanced collectors, thus higher in value. Also the colored glass with white threads is higher than the white with colored threads.

From the collection of Bucky Zelesky.

Gooseberry. Transparent glass is the difference; Clambroths are opaque. All Gooseberrys are rare. I have found several amber, few green and only two blue.

# MICA

Micas. These are simply transparent glass with mica flakes added. They are found clear, blue, green, amber and sometimes red.

# SOLID OPAQUE

Solid Opaques. These marbles are simply solid colored opaque glass. They are found in black, white, blue, green and pink with one or two pontil marks.

# CLAY

Benningtons. These were made of clay and were glazed. They get their name from their resemblance to the pottery made by several manufacturers in Bennington, Vermont. To qualify as being a true Bennington, the marble must have "eyes" or the round spots caused by lying on or against another marble while being fired. The majority of the Bennington marbles found are brown simply because more were made. This is indicated by the way the marbles were packed and shipped. A find of 100 Benningtons in their original box showed a ratio of 75 brown, 20 blue and 5 fancy. This box was also labeled "Made in Germany" which disproves the theory that all "Benningtons" were made in Bennington, Vermont.

Line Crockery. This is another type of marble made of clay. They are usually found in white with zigzag lines of blue or green running randomly around the marble. Sometimes the colors are reversed with the base being colored and the lines white. They are often called "Jaspers" but this is very misleading because they are not made of stone.

Clay. Clay marbles were shaped from clay and hardened in ovens. Some were dyed while others were left their natural colors. The Allbright Company was one of the manufacturers which mass produced this type of marble. When found in their original cloth bags, they are brightly colored. I have found bags of a thousand ½" size and bags of a hundred 1" size. I have also found a large number of ¾" size. The ½" size is most common.

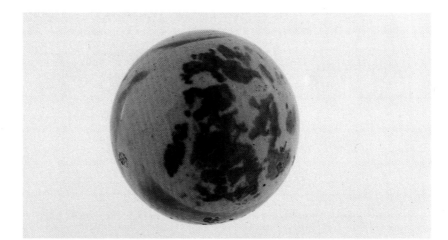

Pottery. Pottery marbles are also made of clay and include the balance of glazed clay marbles which do not fit into the other categories. One of the most common is the tan or light brown which has the colored (usually purple) lines around it. Pottery marbles are also found in a mottled blue and white.

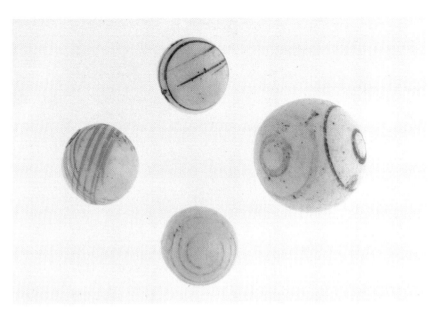

Decorated China, Glazed. Another type of clay marble decorated with lines in a variety of colors running in different directions to form x's, crosses, bulls-eyes and other geometric designs. They are also sometimes decorated with flowers, leaves or stars. There is a great variation in value with the geometric lines being the least expensive, the leaves second, stars third and the flowers most valuable.

Decorated China, Unglazed. This is a fine example of an unglazed china marble, decorated with a strawberry and leaf design.

Decorated China, Unglazed. The three with lines are examples of the geometrics discussed elsewhere. The marble on the far right with the flower is more desirable. The top left with the leaves (or bird tracks as they are sometimes called) would be less desirable.

Decorated China, Glazed. The two bottom are geometric designs. The two top marbles are of more value, being designs of flowers and leaves. Geometrics are valued less.

Decorated China, Unglazed. Geometric and flowers.

Decorated China, Glazed.
This is a nice example of a rose.

Decorated china. Another good example, this one resembling an apple.

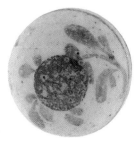

# AGATE

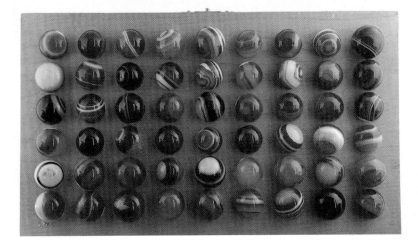

Agates. Agates, or Aggies as they were called, were made from semiprecious stones. The most common was the carnelian, although bloodstone, rose quartz, tiger eyes and others were also used. These marbles also came in solid colors such as black, grey, green, blue and yellow. Some were artificially colored by dying and in some cases the color of the stone was altered by heating. For years these marbles were made by hand. The stone was put to the polishing stone while held between the thumb and forefinger. This polishing left a surface that was rounded by thousands of tiny facets. The facets vary in size, probably indicative of the polisher's expertise. Some can easily be seen with the naked eye; others must be found by looking through a magnifying glass. The newer machine-made Agates do not have these tiny facets.

Six large hand-cut Agates. Top right is a yellow onyx, 2¼" diameter; extreme right, a 2" diameter flint; bottom right, a carnelian, 1⅞" diameter; bottom left, carnelian, 1¼" diameter; far left, green and white dyed agate, ¾" diameter; top left, tiger eye, 1¼" diameter. These marbles are rare in these sizes.

Contemporary Agates and are machine-made.

# COMIC

Comics. Late 20's and 30's. These have possibly been reproduced but I haven't seen any reproductions in the original ⅝" size. A warning that the characters can come off sent me to check all that I had. In some imperfect marbles I found I could scrape the ink off. I have not found a perfect character that could be scraped off. This leads me to believe there may have been discarded marbles that somehow got out of the factory before the last layer of glass was added. There are 12 different characters commonly called a set. They include Skeezix, Ko Ko, Andy, Herbie, Moon, Bimbo, Smitty, Betty Boop, Sandy, Emma, Kayo and Orphan Annie.

A close-up of the Little Orphan Annie marble. This is a nice example of a good marble.

Comic-type marbles, Cotes Bakery and Tom Mix. These two marbles are made in the same manner as the Comics. They have just recently surfaced and not much is known about them. This Tom Mix is the only movie star that has been found as far as I know. The Cotes Bakery is an advertising marble. I have also heard of a marble with a spotted cow on it advertising a dairy as well as a marble that seemed to be made in the same manner which sported an arrow and "5 Cents" on it. There is another with "Vote for Hoover" and still another with an American flag on it. These are extremely rare marbles. I have seen only the Tom Mix and the Cotes Bakery.

# New Comic Type

These marbles have been made recently along with several other types, by more than one company. I have not seen any in the ⅝" size. They have all been larger, ⅞" and up.

We show these for comparison. Skeezix is new, the other five are originals. The test that I have always used is with the blade of my knife. I firmly scrape the figure to see if it will scrape off. I noticed with this test that on the originals I do not feel the figures, as the blade passes over them. On the later marbles, the figures are felt, the ink is much thicker, but it does not scrape off either.

# SULPHIDES

The Sulphides are the most popular of all the types of collectible marbles. Most common are the white animals encased in clear glass. There are also colored figures in clear glass and white figures in colored glass; however, they are scarce and command a premium price from the advanced collector. Other rare and unusual Sulphides include numbers, initials, people, toys and double figures.

Sulphides I have seen include: a rocking horse; alligator; bear standing on hind legs; bear walking, sitting and reclining; cow standing, reclining, and grazing; dogs, many different breeds and positions; elephants; one and two hump camels; llama; deer; buffalo; frog; fish, both one and two; girl in long dress; girl with a doll; boy on stump; baby crying; child praying; child in chair; alligator or lizard on rock; badger; lamb standing, rising, grazing and lying; sheep; eagle on ball; owl; spread eagle; spread owl; lion; pig; squirrel; rabbit; horse grazing and horse rearing; several different birds; crow; chicken; boy and girl; two eagles; two doves; coins; bust of Grover Cleveland, of Dolly Madison and of Jenny Lind; watch; baby in basket; crucifix; Santa Claus; clown; angel and angel praying. Colors of glass I have seen include medium blue, dark blue, green, light amber and dark amber. I have also seen an amethyst color, but it may have just been a clear which had been sun-exposed until it turned. Colored figures I have seen are a spotted dog, and a bird with blue wings and a yellow beak sitting on a green stump.

Sulphides I have heard of, but not seen, include: a train; a ship with full mast; a stagecoach with four horses and leading another one; the American flag; and the bust of Columbus.

In this category, I will give the value of the marble as being a 1¾" specimen in "average near mint" condition.

Sulphide. Bird.

Sulphides. Top left: bird. Top right: owl. Center: eagle. Bottom left: bird. Bottom center: fish. Bottom right: fish.

Sulphides. Children and figures. Bottom row, right: angel.

Sulphides. Animals. Top, dog begging. Left, dog in sitting position. Right, dog. Bottom, cat.

Sulphides. Starting at top center and going clockwise, shown are a pig, horse, sheep, sheep, chicken, goat, sheep, bear.

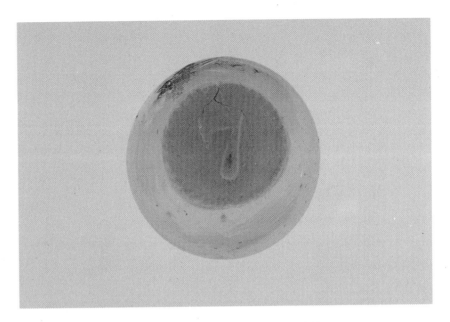

Sulphide. Coin with the numeral 7.

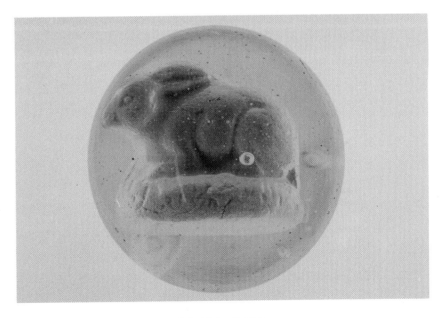

Sulphide. Rabbit.

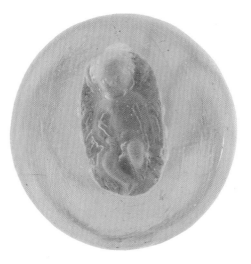

Sulphide. Baby in a basket, sometimes called Moses in the Bullrushes.

Sulphide. Child and dog.

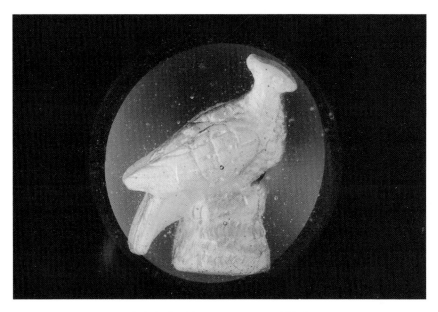

Sulphide. This is an unusual bird.

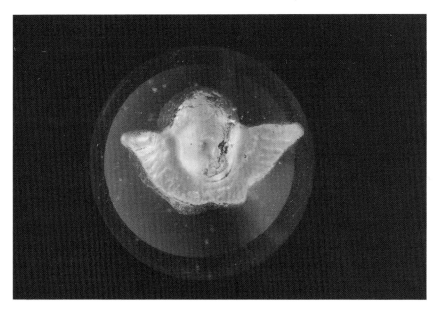

Sulphide. The face of an angel with wings.

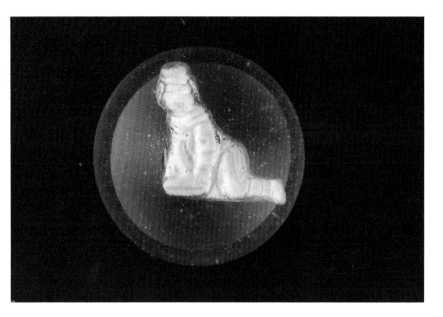

Sulphide. Child in crawling position.

Sulphide. Bird. This particular bird is sometimes called the baby eagle.

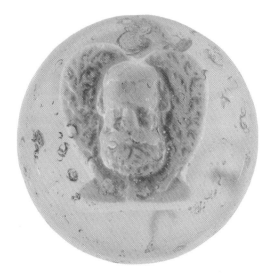

Sulphide. The face of President Garfield, framed by a heart.

The reverse of the President Garfield marble and probably the running mate of the president. The face is obscured by a large bubble.

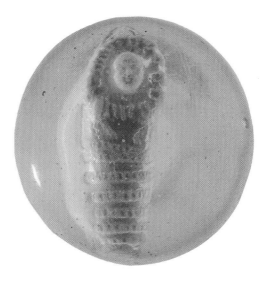

Sulphide. Papoose in a cradle board.

Sulphide. Another papoose in cradle board.

Sulphide. Santa Claus.

Sulphide. Dog with bird in mouth.

Sulphide. Child in a dress.

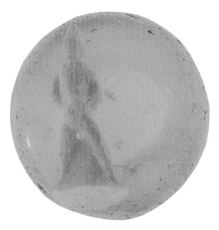

Sulphide. Clown in peaked cap.

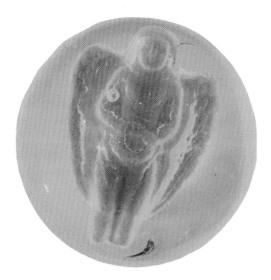

Sulphide. Angel with long wings holding wreath.

Sulphide. Angel with short, flared wings.

Sulphide. Tri-colored Peacock. 1¾"
sold at our 1985 auction for $2,350.00.

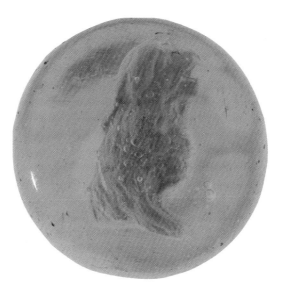

Sulphide. Sitting dog with open mouth.

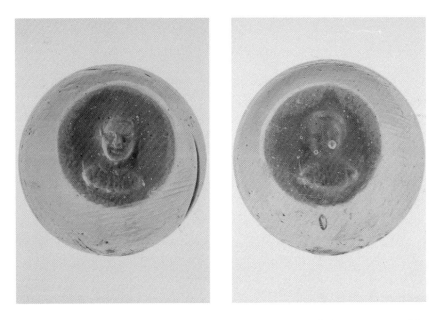

Sulphide. Shown is the obverse and reverse of the same marble showing a coin with two different pictures.

Sulphide. Little Boy Blue.

Sulphide. Crucifix.

Sulphide. Child with hammer.

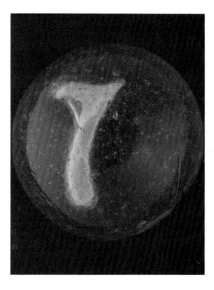

Sulphide. Numerals 7, 4, 2 and 1.

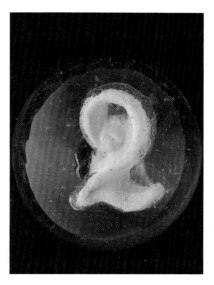

Sulphide. A white sheep in a light amber glass marble.

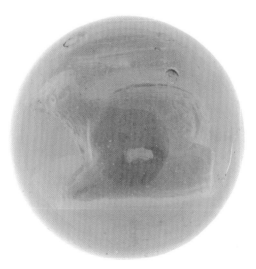

Sulphide. Lamb in a light amber glass marble.

Sulphide. Sheep in a dark amber glass marble. More desirable because of color.

Sulphide. Child in green glass.

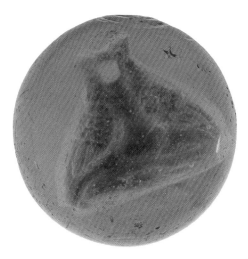

Sulphide. Pair of doves or love birds in blue glass.

Sulphide. A spread-winged owl.

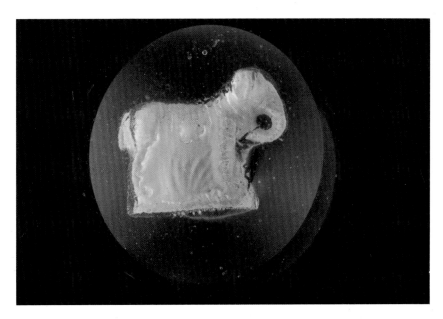

Sulphide. An elephant.

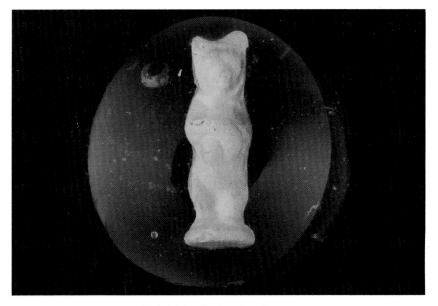

Sulphide. A standing bear.

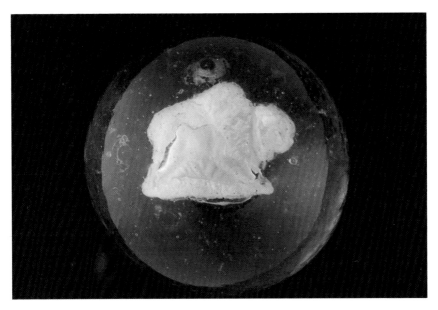

Sulphide. A nice example of an American bison or buffalo.

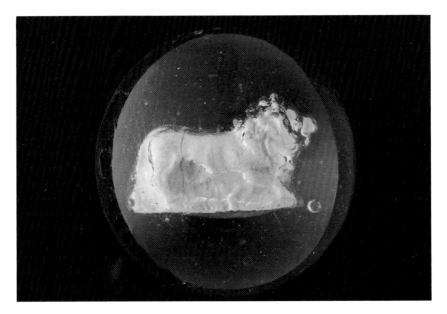

Sulphide. King of the jungle, the lion.

Sulphide Pony. From the collection of Tom and Judy Ecker.

# MACHINE-MADE AND NEW MARBLES

Machine-made marbles are those which were made after the invention of the automatic marble machine. There are many different types and colors, and at the present, most of the advanced collectors are only interested in the ones in the original containers.

While in Florida during the winter of 1982–1983, I discovered a new breed of marble collector. They were boys and girls, generally in the 10 to 15-year-old age range. They have names for many of the machine-made marbles such as Bumblebees, with which I am sure we are all familiar. However, I also heard names like Boy Scout, Bloody Mary, Hurricane, Lightbulb, Cork Screw, Grasshopper, and a few others I can't think of at the present.

I also heard statements like, "Gee, look at this. He is only asking 25 cents for that and it would bring $2.00 on the street." These, then, are the collectors of the future.

I made an attempt to get one of the older boys to sit down with me and pick out and label some of the machine-made marbles; but I was in a mall show and when I had time, he didn't, and vice versa.

Oh, I am sure some of you advanced collectors will laugh, but I predict there is a fortune to be made in machine-made marbles. Remember though, in my lifetime, I have heard the Early American glass collectors of the 1930's and 1940's laugh at the Tiffany and Art Glass collectors. The Tiffany and Art Glass collectors of the 1950's and 1960's laugh at the Carnival glass collectors, and the Carnival glass collectors of the 1960's and 1970's laugh at the Depression glass collectors, but who's laughing now!

New Marbles. The bulk of this collection of new marbles was made by the Joe St. Clair Glass Company of Elwood, Indiana. The exceptions are the two marbles on the left in the bottom row, which were produced by a glass studio in California. All are approximately 2" in diameter and are indicative of the fine art work presently going into the manufacture of marbles.

This collection of marbles shows the unique coloring which gives rise to the names of Bumblebees and Black Widows.

An original game box containing the metal playing plate. This game by Girard Toys is called the American Marble Game. Marbles are not original. I have seen these plates before but never in their original box.

A box of "Akro Solitary Checkers" marbles and game board. Not an extremely rare item.

Machine-made Marbles. This design is called Cork Screw because the color starts at one place on the marble and runs around it at least one time completely without crossing or touching.

# SLAG

Slag. A large amber slag machine-made marble.

Slag. A fine collection of early machine-made slag marbles in red, blue, green and amber. The glass rolling pin is a unique way of displaying marbles.

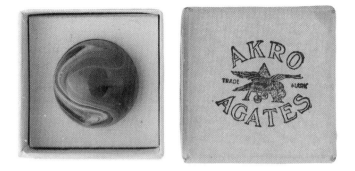

Slag. This is a wonderful red slag marble still in its box marked "Akro Agates." This item would be of interest to both marble collectors as well as Akro Agate collectors. This is a unique item, one I have not had the good fortune to have seen before. Marbles and related objects, such as the original packing box, game board, etc., which seem to be one-of-a-kind objects cannot be valued objectively. It must be between the buyer and seller to come to an understanding as to what one will give and what the other will accept as a fair market value. Rare.

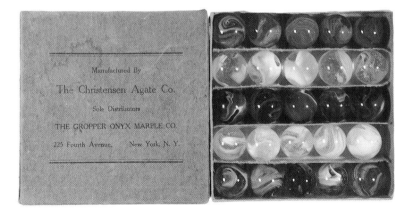

Slag. A boxful of machine-made slag marbles in their original container. These were manufactured by the Christensen Agate Company.

Popeye Akro Agate box containing 15 tri-color cork screws and marble bag.

Box of 25 Akro Agate Imperials. I have also seen a box of this type (different marbles of course) labeled Carnelian Agates. I doubt if the present day truth-in-advertising laws would let them get by with this.

Akro Agate box. Marbles are not original. Center section should contain either bag or knee pad.

Box of Akro Agates and marble bag.

A metal box containing Akro Agate marbles with rules and bag.

Showing top of box.

This ends the section of marbles covered in the Updated Values. The marbles that follow are either one-of-a-kind or so rare that one is seldom sold or, in some cases, prices are stated on similar marbles earlier in this book.

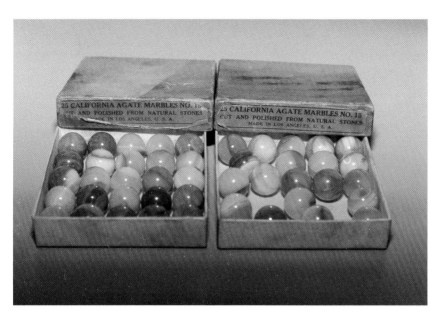

Two boxes of 25 American made Agates. From the collection of Tom and Judy Ecker. Rare.

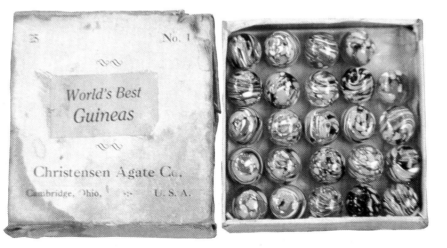

Box of 24 (one missing) hand-made marbles. Christensen Agate Co. Rare. From the collection of Gary and Sally Dolly.

# ODDITIES

A fine example of the pontil mark on a marble.

The opposite end of the same marble.

A collection of Transparent Swirls, a couple of Opaque Swirls and a couple of Micas. All peewees, these marbles measure ½" in diameter or less.

Goldstones are not really stone but glass with copper flakes all over, the same as streaks in Lutz-type marbles. I never saw one with pontil marks so I don't know how or when they were made. They are very attractive and most collectors share them.

# RARITIES

11/16" Decorated chinas unglazed. These were sold at our 1985 auction.

End of Day, Onionskin and Opaque Swirl Lutz. Probably from same cane. All three 13/16".

Box of Master Made Marbles from early 1930's.

Reverse of box giving the rules for playing ringer.

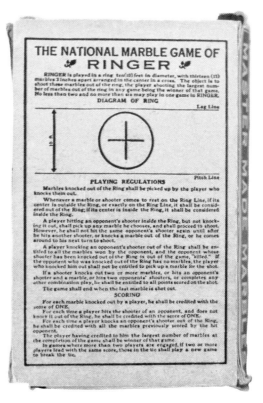

THE NATIONAL MARBLE GAME OF
RINGER

RINGER is played in a ring ten(10) feet in diameter, with thirteen (13) marbles 3 inches apart arranged in the center in a cross. The object is to shoot these marbles out of the ring, the player shooting the largest number of marbles out of the ring in any game being the winner of that game. No less than two and no more than six may play in one game in RINGER.

DIAGRAM OF RING

PLAYING REGULATIONS

Marbles knocked out of the Ring shall be picked up by the player who knocks them out.

Whenever a marble or shooter comes to rest on the Ring Line, if its center is outside the Ring, or exactly on the Ring Line, it shall be considered out of the Ring; if its center is inside the Ring, it shall be considered inside the Ring.

A player hitting an opponent's shooter inside the Ring, but not knocking it out, shall pick up any marble he chooses, and shall proceed to shoot. However, he shall not hit the same opponent's shooter again until after he hits another shooter, or knocks a marble out of the Ring, or he comes around to his next turn to shoot.

A player knocking an opponent's shooter out of the Ring shall be entitled to all the marbles won by the opponent, and the opponent whose shooter has been knocked out of the Ring is out of the game, "killed." If the opponent who was knocked out of the Ring has no marbles, the player who knocked him out shall not be entitled to pick up a marble for the shot.

If a shooter knocks out two or more marbles, or hits an opponent's shooter and a marble, or hits two opponents' shooters, or completes any other combination play, he shall be entitled to all points scored on the shot.

The game shall end when the last marble is shot out.

SCORING

For each marble knocked out by a player, he shall be credited with the score of ONE.

For each time a player hits the shooter of an opponent, and does not knock it out of the Ring, he shall be credited with the score of ONE.

For each time a player knocks an opponent's shooter out of the Ring, he shall be credited with all the marbles previously scored by the hit opponent.

The player having credited to him the largest number of marbles at the completion of the game shall be winner of that game.

In games where more than two players are engaged, if two or more players lead with the same score, those in the tie shall play a new game to break the tie.

Stone marbles, none of which were available at the photographing session, are some of the earliest marbles. They are reported to have been found in the mounds built by the prehistoric people of North America along with artifacts indicating that those early inhabitants played other games as well. We should remember that the word "marble" itself was derived from the little ball made from marble and alabaster during the Roman empire. Lucky is the person who would have one of these little museum quality gems in their collection; but, I'm afraid we are not likely to come into contact with this type today. We will have to be content with the fairly plentiful marbles which are the ones made in Germany during the nineteenth century. They are both white and grey and sometimes dyed. They are of little value but are often included in the marble collections so as to make the whole more complete.

Steel marbles or steelies are another type we failed to photograph. The type most often seen are really just ball bearings which have been nickel plated but actually there was a steel marble manufactured. It is hollow and has a cross on one side where the steel comes together. They are scarce.

Carpet balls are not really marbles but are included here because most marble collections contain at least one. Made of porcelain, these balls were used in England and Scotland to play a game. This game was played in the house on the carpet, hence the name "carpet balls." The set includes 12 larger balls and one small one about 2½" in diameter. We are not sure how the game was played.

Gift box. The Bowtie, Bullet Pencil and Akro Agates fit into respective lots. From the collection of Gary and Sally Dolly. Rare.

16-lobed Onionskin 2" size, also nice 2" Clambroth. From the collection of Gary and Sally Dolly.

General Grant game board with 32 Transparent Swirls. From the collection of Mark Howard.

Unusual red one-pontil marble. 1⅝". From the collection of Mark Howard.

Glazed China Pink Rose. ⅞". From the collection of Mark Howard.

General grant game board with variety of 1" marbles. Two pontils, one pontil, and no pontils. From the collection of Carol Smith.

Not of much value but a beautiful photograph. See what a little imagination can do. From the collection of Carol Smith.

Sulfide. 2⅝", with three separate figures: cat, duck and fish. From the collection of David Terren.

Hand-painted China. 1⅜". From the collection of Stan Block.

Large green and yellow solid inner core with two opposite outer layers of red and white flanked by two clear glass with mica panels. From the collection of Gordon Jones.

Beautiful multi-colored Onionskin with loads of mica. From the collection of Gordon Jones.

Clambroth. ¾" to ⅞". From the collection of Stan Block.

Dyed Agates. ⅝" to ⅞". From the collection of Stan Block.

Three-colored ribbons coming from base and ending at sides. One pontil, $9/16$". From the collection of Tom and Judy Ecker.

Hand-painted China. $11/16$". Outstanding. From the collection of Tom and Judy Ecker.

Beautiful, hand-painted Chinas. $5/8$" to $7/8$". From the collection of Tom and Judy Ecker.

Lined crockery. Notice normal green and blue, reversed green and white and white with green, blue and red, ¹¹⁄₁₆" to ¹³⁄₁₆". From the collection of Tom and Judy Ecker.

Unusual Banded Opaques. From the collection of Tom and Judy Ecker.

Four-lobed Onionskin. Note depth of lobes, 2¹⁄₁₆". From the collection of Tom and Judy Ecker.

Horizontal Swirl. Handmade, ¹⁵⁄₁₆". From the collection of Tom and Judy Ecker.

Nice hand-painted China. ¹⁵⁄₁₆". From the collection of D. Logan, Clinton, B.C.

Three panels of red and white Onionskin spearated by clear glass showing core of mica. From the collection of Jim and Louise O'Connell.

Beautiful collection of Lutz. From the collection of Carol Smith.

On the following pages are pictures of part of Jim Moeller's collection. To save space I will withhold useless comment. Enjoy them.

Two of the finest marbles I have ever seen. 1¼" Green Glass Lutz and 1⅞" Clambroth Blue with white lines.

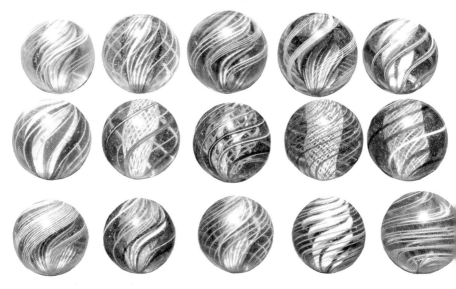

Moeller's Collection.

Moeller's Collection.

Moeller's Collection.

Moeller's Collection.

Moeller's Collection.

Moeller's Collection.

Moeller's Collection.

## TRANSPARENT SWIRL

pg. 9 Solid Core Swirl - ⅝" ......................$35.00
  1¾" ........................................$275.00
pg. 10 Divided Core Swirl - ⅝" .................$50.00
  1¾" ........................................$250.00
pg. 11 Latticino Core Swirl - ⅝" .................$30.00
  1¾" ........................................$225.00
  Ribbon Core - ⅝" ...........................$75.00
  1¾" ........................................$450.00
pg. 12 Lobed Core Swirl - ⅝" ....................$75.00
  1¾" ........................................$400.00
  Coreless Swirl - ⅝" .........................$20.00
  1¾" ........................................$250.00
pg. 13 Transparent Swirl (Ribbon Core)
  ⅝" .........................................$120.00
  (Solid Core) - 1¾" .........................$800.00
pg. 14 (Solid Core) - 1¾" .........................$425.00
  (Split or Divided Core) - 1¾" .........$300.00

## LUTZ

pg. 15 Clear Swirl - ⅝" .............................$125.00
  1¾" ........................................$900.00
pg. 16 Colored Transparent Swirl ⅝" .......$225.00
  1¾" .......................................$2,700.00
  Opaque Glass Swirls - ⅝" .............$325.00
  1¾" .......................................$5,000.00
pg. 17 Ribbon Core Lutz - ⅝" .................$300.00
  1¾" .......................................$3,500.00
  Onionskin Lutz - ⅝" ......................$275.00
  1¾" .......................................$2,350.00
pg. 18 Single Color Lutz - ⅝" ..................$300.00
  1¾" .......................................$2,200.00
  Indian Swirl - ⅝" ...........................$450.00
  1¾" .......................................$4,500.00
pg. 19 Onionskin Lutz - 1¾" ................$2,500.00
  Green Single Color ⅝" .................$450.00
pg. 20 Clear Glass Lutz - 1¾" .................$900.00
  Ribbon Core Lutz - ⅝" .................$300.00
  1¾" .......................................$3,500.00
pg. 21 Opaque Swirl Lutz - ⅝" ...............$375.00

## PEPPERMINT SWIRL

  Peppermint Swirls - ⅝" .................$100.00
  1¾" .......................................$3,500.00
pg. 22 Peppermint Swirls with mica -
  ⅝" .........................................$500.00
  1¾" .......................................$3,500.00
pg. 23 **INDIAN SWIRL** - ⅝" .......................$85.00
  1¾" .......................................$2,500.00
  360° Indian Swirl ⅝" ....................$400.00
  Joseph Swirl ⅝" ..........................$300.00

## BANDED OPAQUE SWIRL

pg. 24 Banded Opaque Swirls - ⅝" ..........$150.00
  1¾" .......................................$2,200.00

## BANDED TRANSPARENT SWIRL -

  ⅝" .........................................$100.00
  1¾" .......................................$1,000.00
  Amber with yellow ⅝" ...................$75.00
  May be Leighton Marble 1¼" .............Rare

## ONIONSKIN

pg. 26 Onionskin - 1¾" ..........................$500.00
pg. 27 Onionskin (16 lobed) - 1¾" .......$1,900.00

Onionskin (unusual coloring)
  1¾" ........................................$900.00
pg. 28 Onionskin (four lobed) - 1¾" .....$1,400.00
  Nice Specimen 1¾" ....................$500.00
pg. 29 Another Nice Specimen 1¾" ........$500.00
  Onionskin with mica - ⅝" .............$100.00
  1¾" .......................................$1,200.00
pg. 30 1¾" .......................................$1,200.00
pg. 31 **OPAQUE SWIRL** - ⅝" ....................$50.00
  1¾" ........................................$800.00
  **END OF DAY** - 1¾" ...................$1,200.00
pg. 32 **CLAMBROTH** - ⅝" ......................$225.00
  1¾" .......................................$2,400.00
pg. 33 Gooseberry ⅝" ...........................$150.00
  **MICAS** - ⅝" ...................................$30.00
  1¾" ........................................$650.00
  True Red ⅝" ................................$800.00
pg. 34 **SOLID OPAQUES** - ⅝" ...................$35.00
  1¾" ........................................$800.00

## CLAY

  Benningtons - ⅝" (brown and blue) ..$1.00
  ⅝" (fancy) ...................................$3.00
  1¾" (brown and blue)...............$30.00
  1¾" (fancy) .................................$50.00
pg. 35 Line Crockery - ⅝" .........................$15.00
  1¾" ........................................$175.00
pg. 36 Clay - ⅝" ......................................$.50
  1¾" ..........................................$5.00
  Pottery - ⅝" ................................$5.00
  1¾" ..........................................$75.00
pg. 37 Decorated China, Glazed
  Lines ⅝" ....................................$25.00
  1¾" ........................................$175.00
  Strawberry & Leaves 1¾" ............$450.00
pg. 38 Decorated China, Unglazed
  Lines ⅝" ....................................$15.00
  Flower 1¾" .................................$475.00
pg. 39 Geometric & Flowers
  ⅝" .........................................$100.00
  1¾" ........................................$350.00
  Decorated China, Glazed (rose) -
  ⅝" .........................................$350.00
  1¾" .......................................$2,100.00
  Decorated China (apple) - ⅝" ........$300.00
  1¾" .......................................$1,200.00

## AGATE

pg. 40 Carnelian (with bulls-eye & one ring)
  ⅝" ...........................................$30.00
  1¾" ........................................$175.00
pg. 41 Contemporary Agates - ⅝" .............$3.00
  1¾" .........................................$35.00

## COMIC (Late 20s and 30s)

pg. 42 Skeezix ......................................$100.00
  Herbie.......................................$100.00
  Smitty .......................................$110.00
  Emma ........................................$85.00
  Ko Ko........................................$100.00
  Moon.........................................$275.00
  Betty.........................................$275.00
  Kayo .........................................$375.00

Andy ............................................ $85.00
Bimbo ............................................ $90.00
Sandy ............................................ $90.00
Annie ............................................ $100.00

**COMIC - TYPE**

pg. 43 Tom Mix ................................ $2,500.00
Cotes Bakery ............................ $1,200.00
pg. 44 New Comic Type .................. each $10.00

**SULPHIDES - (Animals)**

pg. 45 Bird - 1¾" .................................. $300.00
pg. 46 Bird - 1¾" .................................. $200.00
Owl - 1¾" ...................................... $250.00
Eagle - 1¾" .................................... $300.00
Bird - 1¾" ...................................... $200.00
Fish - 1⅓" ...................................... $200.00
Fish - 1¾" ...................................... $200.00

**CHILDREN & ANGEL FIGURES** .......... each $650.00

pg. 47 Dog begging - 1¾" ...................... $175.00
Dog sitting - 1¾" ............................ $175.00
Dog - 1¾" ...................................... $175.00
Cat - 1¾" ...................................... $175.00
Pig - 1¾" ...................................... $175.00
Horse - 1¾" .................................. $175.00
Sheep - 1¾" .................................. $175.00
Sheep - 1¾" .................................. $175.00
Rooster - 1¾" ................................ $175.00
Goat - 1¾" .................................... $175.00
Sheep - 1¾" .................................. $175.00
Bear - 1¾" .................................... $175.00
pg. 48 Coin with numeral 7 - 1¾" ............ $750.00
Rabbit - 1¾" .................................. $250.00
pg. 49 Baby in a basket - 1¾" .................. $800.00
Child and dog - 1¾" .................... $1,000.00
pg. 50 Unusual Bird - 1¾" ...................... $300.00
Face of angel with wings - 1¾" .. $1,000.00
pg. 51 Child crawling - 1¾" ...................... $600.00
Bird (baby eagle) 1¾" .................... $350.00
pg. 52 Pres. Garfield - 1¾" .................... $1,200.00
pg. 53 Papoose - 1¾" .............................. $800.00
Papoose - 1¾" .............................. $800.00
pg. 54 Santa Claus - 1¾" ...................... $1,300.00
Dog with bird in mouth - 1¾" .... $1,100.00
pg. 55 Child in a dress - 1¾" .................... $600.00
Clown in peaked cap - 1¾" ........ $1,000.00
pg. 56 Angel with wreath - 1¾" .............. $750.00
Angel with short wings - 1¾" ....... $750.00
pg. 57 Tri-colored peacock - 1¾" .......... $8,000.00
Dog with open mouth - 1¾" ......... $300.00
pg. 58 Coin - 1¾" .................................. $750.00
Little Boy Blue - 1¾" .................... $750.00
pg. 59 Crucifix - 1¾" .............................. $650.00
Child with hammer - 1¾" ............ $600.00
pg. 60 Numerals 7, 4, 2, and 1 - 1¾" ... each $500.00
pg. 61 Sheep in light amber marble - 1¾" .................................. $2,000.00
Lamb in light amber marble - 1¾" .................................. $2,000.00
pg. 62 Sheep in dark amber marble - 1¾' .................................. $2,000.00
Child in green glass - 1¾" .......... $4,000.00
pg. 63 Love birds - 1¾" ........................ $5,000.00
Spread-winged owl - 1¾" ............ $350.00
pg. 64 Elephant - 1¾' ............................ $300.00
Standing Bear - 1¾" .................... $200.00
pg. 65 American Bison - 1¾" .................. $300.00
Lion - 1¾" .................................... $300.00
pg. 66 Pony - 1¾" .................................. $200.00
pg. 67 New Marbles - 2" .......................... $40.00
pg. 68 Bumblebees & Black Widows... each $2.00
American Marble Game .............. $110.00
pg. 69 Akro Solitary checkers .................. $75.00
Machine-made corkscrew ... average $4.00
pg. 70 **SLAG** - 1¾" .................................. $150.00
Slag Marbles ........... each $2.00 to $10.00
Rolling Pin .................................... $18.00
pg. 71 Red slag in box .......................... $800.00
Christensen Agate in box .......... $1,250.00
pg. 72 Popeye Akro Agate in box ........ $2,500.00
25 Akro Agate Imperials ........... $1,200.00
pg. 73 Akro Agate box only .................. $150.00
Box Akro Agates & marble bag .... $900.00
pg. 74 Metal box with Akro Agate marbles, rules & bag .............................. $2,000.00
pg. 75 Guineas .................................... $6,000.00
pg. 76 For example only
pg. 77 Transparent Swirls vary in value from $6.00 for the common Latticino Core to $10.00 for the Mica, and up to $35.00 for the Opaque Swirls.
Goldstones - ¾' .............................. $20.00
Goldstones - 1¾" .......................... $45.00
pg. 78 Top photo ............................ each $200.00
Middle ................................ each $400.00
Bottom photo, all three sold at 1985 auction for .................................. $975.00
pg. 79 Box of marbles sold at 1985 auction for .............................................. $10.00
pg. 80 Carpet Balls .................. $125.00 – 300.00
pgs. 81 – 93 ...No prices available. These items are rare, one-of-a-kind, or pictured elsewhere in the book.